JN438325

종달새

The Lark

● 번역 | 라이채(Eechae Ra)

번역작가
덕성여대 영문과 졸업
미연방 한의사
한국문인 편집주간 및 번역책임자 역임
한국문인번역대상 수상
찰스 부룩스의 『유머와 위트의 차이』(국역),
이철호 소설집, 권남희 수필집, 안명희 기행수필집, 이택화 시집, 송양의 시집 영역 외 다수의 역서

B.A., English Language and Literature, Duksung Women's Univ.
Managing Translator of Korea Writers
Certificated Acupuncturist and Herbologist in the U.S.A
Korea Writers Winner for Excellent Translation
Translated On the Difference Between Wit and Humor
by Charles Brooks (English into Korean),
Collection of Chul-Ho Lee's Novels,
Collections of Taek-Wha Lee and Yang-Eui' Song's Poems,
Collections of Nam-Hee Kwon and Myung-Hee Ahn's Essays
(Korean into English), and etc.

● 감수 | 자넬 리브(Janell Reeve)

다수의 영한대역작품들을 감수함
미국 워싱턴 주 시애틀에 거주
산호세대학 졸업
2008-2009년 한국에서 예수그리스도후기성도교회의 선교사로 봉사함

She has proofread many English and Korean literary works
Living in a suburb of Seattle, Washington in the United States
Graduated from San Jose State University
Did missionary work in Korea for the Church of Jesus Christ of Latter-day Saints from 2008 to 2009

종달새

The Lark

이 독 밀 한영대역시집

Lee Dok-mill

도서출판 천우

감자의 꿈

내 꿈은 노벨문학상,
나는 노벨문학상을 꿈꾸지만
노력하지 않는다면
나는 구제받지 못한다.

나는 나의 그림자와 사각의 링에서 결투한다.

꿈 따라 30여 년, 하늘에 북극성이 제자리를 잃어버릴 수는 있을지라도 내꿈은 변하지 않는다.

내가 처한 현실에서 운명을 극복하고, 쓰러지지 않으려는 안간힘이 나를 꿈꾸게 하였고, 그 수많은 언어 중에서 유독 어리석은 말 몇 개를 골라 내 마음에 밭을 갈고 씨를 뿌렸다.

씨눈 감자를 심어 감자에서 싹이 나고 잎이 나고 그리고 열매(열매라고 해두자)맺고…. 호미로 더듬어 밭을 일구어 보면 조랑조랑 주렁주렁, 주저리주저리 뿌리에 매달려 호밋새로 헤집고 얼굴 내민다. 비로소 해를 보는 것이다.

작은 씨감자를 꿈으로 사랑으로 노력으로 가꾸어주

면 얼마나 귀엽고 사랑스런 모습이냐!

그 작은 씨감자 조각에서 엄청난 감자알들이 만들어져 나오는 것은 굳이 감자뿐만이 아니리라.

인간이기 때문에 운명이 있는 것이 아니다.

인간이기 때문에 운명을 극복하려 노력할 수 있다고 생각하지도 말라. 저 흙 속의 감자 알갱이들도 저마다 크고 좋은 알갱이들이 되기 위하여 땅 속에서 일정 기간 꿈꾸며 싸우며 기다려 왔을 것이다.

그리고 드디어 해를 만났다.

그리고 우리들의 맛있는 감자가 되어 먹어지고 또 사라지는 것…

한 사람, 한 사람, 한 사람… 우리들의 인생 역정도 마찬가지라 생각된다.

나도 해를 만나고 싶다.

나도 지금 저 땅 속의 꿈틀대는 감자알처럼

내 마음 속에 큰 감자가 되고 싶어 꿈틀대는 마그마가 끓고 있다.

2014. 2. 28.

Kyeong

A Dream of Potatoes

My dream is the Nobel Prize,
I dream the Nobel Prize,
But if I don't try for it,
I cannot be saved.

I fight a duel against my shadow in the square ring.

Though the pole star in the sky lost its position, my dream didn't change any for 30 years more.

Overcoming my destiny in this present situation, and holding back an urge not to fall down, I dreamed of it by it. I plowed the field of my mind and planted a few silly words chosen from among lots of languages.

At first when I planted one of the seed potatoes, it wasn't long before the new eyes sprouted, its petals came out, and it finally produced fruits (let's say 'the fruit'). When we cleared the field using a weeding hoe, lots of the fruits stuck out their faces from where the hoe was dangling over the clusters of roots. At last they faced the sun.

I cultivated only one of the small seed potatoes by my dream, love, and effort before I saw what fine and lovcly results they were!

The fact that enormous numbers of potatoes come out of a small seed potato is not confined to the case of only this potato.

Destiny doesn't exist because we are human beings.

Don't think that we can try to overcome destiny because we are human beings. The seeds of potatoes that went into that soil would have waited, dreaming and fighting, in order to become a fine or big potato for a definite period of time.

And at last they met the sun.

They become our delicious prey and were returned to soil…; a man (a person), a man, a man, I think, has the same course of life.

I wish to meet the sun.

In my mind the magma is boiling to become a big potato, as if their seeds are wiggling into that ground.

2014. 2. 28.

Kyeong 송

나의 사랑하는 도깨비 아저씨

나는 이 시집을
나의 조국과, 내가 힘들고 아팠을 때
나를 따뜻하게 돌봐주신 나의 약혼자(fiancé),
도깨비 아저씨(ghost)께 드립니다.

To my beloved ghost

I dedicate these poems to my country,
and my fiancé, who helps me warmly
when I was ill as weakable heart.

제1부

제2부

제3부

제4부

제 1 부

아고라 스케치

붉은 개스등이 새벽안개에 녹는
거리를 가로질러 그리 깊지 않은 바다에 들면(入)
아직 이른 서해가 정작 그릴 날(日)보다 붉다

어느 신(神)이
문처럼 발치에 심은 등을 끄자
꿈을 꾸면서 사람들이 화안하고 명랑한 얼굴로
집을 나선다 한 손에 활과
어깨엔 기타를 메고

시대가 평화로운 이곳에서는
시민과 종이가 혼돈을 벗고
오!
나는 희랍인
옛 시인의 달콤한 입술로
향내 그윽한
노래를 불렀다

| 시작 노트 |

Agora 광장 : 인하대학교 도서관이 있는 광장. '생각하는 사람' 동상이 있음. 새벽에 학생들이 등교하는 정경 묘사.

–1983. 7.

Agora Sketch

When we step in the sea not very deep,
Crossing thc street about where the gas light melts in dawn's fog,
The early western sea is really redder to paint than during the day.

When any god
Puts out the lamp in the vicinity of the gate,
People leave home, dreams showing in their bright and cheerful faces
With a bow in one hand
And a guitar on a shoulder.

In this peaceful place at this time,
Citizens and papers are in confusion,
Oh!
I sang an aromatic song
With the sweet lips
Of an old Greek poet.

| Note |
Agora Square : It's an open space in which the library of Inha Univ. is situated and the statue of 'a thinking man' is built there.

–1983. 7.

하늘 길

그대의 하늘 길을 나는 알아요
오늘도 나의 작은 창에
등불이 꺼지지 않는 까닭은

달은 달이 가는 길이 있고
지구는 지구가 가는 길이 있고
왕은 왕이 가는 길이 있고
사람은 저마다
마땅히 가야 할 나만의 길이
있기 때문이지요.

매일 매일이 똑같이 반복되는
일상일지라도
나의 소망의 씨앗은
깊은 바다 속에서 끓고 있는 마그마처럼
두근거리는 내 심정 안에
숨어 있습니다.

그대가 잠든 내 머리 위으로
하늘 길을 달려와
나의 꿈속에서 속삭이면
나의 길은,

깜깜한 모래 먼지 자욱하여
선인의 발자취도 찾을 수 없고,

바람이 불 때마다 앞길을
잃어버리는 사하라 사막에서도
오직
하늘 길에서 반짝이며 날 인도하는
북극성과 같은 그대의
사랑 때문인 것을 나는 알아요
오아시스를 발견하듯 일상의 먼지 속에서 그대의
기도를 찾을 수 있다면 나는 그대로 인하여
죽는 날까지 별을 노래하는
시인의 길을 가리라 약속합니다
나의 길은
그대가 날 찾아오시는
하늘 길의 곡선과 어울리는
파동을 가졌습니다.

| 시작 노트 |
꼭두새벽 하늘에 형형히 빛나는 정찰위성을 바라보며 공부를 한다.

The Heavenly Way(The Satellite)

I know your heavenly way,
The reason why the lamp doesn't die out
In my little window today.

There is a way the moon revolves around,
The way the earth revolves around,
The way the king goes,
And the only way for each one
That humans ought to go.

Even though it is
The everyday life,
Repeating consistently day by day,
My hope's seed.
Like the magma boiling into the deep sea,
Hides in a throbbing heart.

Above my head you slept
When you rushed through the heavenly way,
And whispered in my dream,
My way,
Hiding with black dust,
Cannot be found even in the predecessors' track,

And each time the wind blows,
Even in the Sahara desert, losing the way to go.
Only
I know your love
Like Polaris leading my way
Twinkling in the way of heaven.
If I find your prayer in daily dusts like finding an oasis,
I can promise the way of singing to a star
Until the last day because of you.
My way
Has a wave motion
Becoming well from the heavenly curve
That you search for me.

| Note |
I always study in the dark before the dawn, looking up at the light of the reconnaissance satellite.

인연(因緣)

그대는 난초와 같이 고결하고
섬세하며, 그대는 사막의 선인장처럼 또한
뜨거운 열정의 화관을 쓰고 있구나.

몸에는 만 가지 향취가
그대 머리 위로 오색 후광을 만들었으니
때로는 잠깐 빛남도 저 하늘의
샛별 같아라.

나만의 그대,
그대와 나의 연분의 정(情)도
한 개 떨어질 꽃잎으로 여겨질지라도
그대 향한 사모의 마음일랑
지옥의 불화로보다 더 뜨겁게
타올라,

그대와 내가
이별해야 한다면

차라리 내 몸을 불길에 사르고
그대의 오묘한 오색 후광 속에서
더욱 빛나는
찬란한 금관으로
되어지고 싶구나.

Karma

You are as noble, as delicate as an orchid,
And have a hot passionate flowery crown on your head
Like a cactus in the desert.

With ten thousand perfumes about your body,
As you formed a rainbow halo above your head,
Sometimes the instant glow
Is as bright as the morning star.

You are the only one for me,

Even though the curious feeling of connection between you and I
Is supposed to fall as a flower,
My heart's longing for you
Burns hotter than hell's fire,

But if you and I
Have to say goodbye,

I would rather put my body into fire,
And wish to become a brilliant gold crown,
Shining brighter
In your secret rainbow halo.

고해성사

나 그대 몰랐던들
십자가를 알았을까

나 그대 알았으나
캄캄한 안개 속에 반짝이는
십자성을 알았을까

봄 여름 가고
기나긴 겨울이 오면
명경같이 차가운 하늘가에
그칠 줄 모르는 모정의 밤이어라

나 그대 몰랐으나
어둠 속에 반짝이는 그 별 하나

눈시울에 적셔 우는
슬픔의 탄식을 왜 몰랐을까

나 그대 몰랐던들
십자성을 찾았을까

| 시작 노트 |
십자성은 하느님의 존재하심.

My Confession

If I did not know you
Could I know the cross?

Though I knew you,
Could I know the twinkling Cross-star
In the dark?

The spring and summer has passed
When the long winter comes,

At the edge of sky, as cold as a mirror,
The longing's night is ceaseless.

Though I did not know you,
The one star glimmers into the darkness,

Why didn't I know
Its sorrow's lamentation moving me to tears?

If I didn't know you,
Could I find the Cross-star?

| Note |
The Cross-star means the existence of God.

그대에게로

너와 내가 쌓는 이 성이
모래성일지라도 먼 바다를 꿈꾸는
수부들을 싣고 너울거리며 파도가
우리의 성을 덮칠지라도

하늘도 알고 땅도 알아버린 가난한
연인들을 위해 아침엔 금빛 찬란히
돛을 물들이면서 거기 머 언 나라로 가면

이 모래성이 필시 파도에 묻힐지라도
우리의 사랑도 이 바다 어느 항구로든
마침내 당도하리

To You

If this castle,
Being built by you and me,
Was sand,
If the castle was hit
By a wave rolling about the fishermen's feet,

If these lovers, so poor as to be known
To the air and the ground,
Fly to a far-away land
On the misted morning's golden light;

If the sandcastle was covered by the waves,
Our love would be anchored in a harbor
At last.

당신 곁에

새벽 동산 위
나는, 떠오르는 광명한 태양
나는 태양의 그림자

태양의 흑점 속에
까맣게 타버린 한 점(占)
나는 태양의 그림자

서산에 넘어가는
일몰의 기다린 나의 그림자
당신의 나는 그림자

그리고
또한 당신은
깜깜한 밤
나만의 사당에 타오르는
촛불 아래 너무도 기-ㄴ
나의 그림자

당신 곁에 가만히 앉아
한 오리 연기로 화해버릴
나와 똑같은
당신은 나의 그림자
당신은 나의 그림자

I Am Beside You

Above the mountain at dawn
I am the bright rising sun,
I am the shadow of it.

One spot, burned black
In that sunspot,
I am the shadow of the sun.

It's my long shadow
That is sinking in the west mountain,
In you I am a shadow.

And
Also you
Are very long shadow of me,
In the deep night, under the candle
Burning up in the shrine
Only for me.

You are my shadow,
You are my shadow
The same as me,
As I sit silently at your side,
To transform into a wisp of smoke.

태어난 땅

설악산령에는 기막히게 큰 눈사태도
돌덩이처럼 굴러 떨어지지 아니하고
그곳에 모두 모아 폭포수 되어 오노라 가노라
계절을 되풀이하느니

안개구름 자욱하다
어디엔가 동해바다 무인도 흰 물새 소리
돌아앉은 망부석조차 귓전에 소란탠다
두 손 들어 귀막이를 하는구나

외할미는 에미 잃은 손녀딸 손목 잡고
자주 등대에 와서,
찰박찰박 홀로 초록빛 고운 물에
바닷가재 따라드니

동트는 새벽부터
해 넘어가는 수평선을 보며 아이는
까닭 모를 슬픔을 느꼈구나
할미 손 잡혀 집으로 오는 길에

할머니 왜 나만 혼자 여기 있어?
으응,

니 에민 저 바다 건너
해뜨는 나라로 갔단다
아니 해 지는 곳이랬나

아이는 그 후 하루도 빠짐없이
동해 바다 검푸른 물에
용트림하며 솟아오르는
해돋이를 바라보며 자라더니

먼 훗날, 어느 시끄러운 아침 저자에
우뚝이 차가운 기상으로
어리둥실 떠올랐더라

The Birthplace

In the Seorak mountains the amazingly big avalanche
Didn't fall down like stones
And make a waterfall pool there,
Showing us the repeated seasons, coming and going.

The mist clouds are thick.
The cries of white water birds heard somewhere in an uninhabited island of the east sea
Are noisy even to a deceased husband's ears,
And make her cover her ears with two hands.

A grandmother took a granddaughter by her hands, grieving for her mother
And often came to the lighthouse.
Then making the water sound into the green clear seawater,
She alone plays hide–and–seek with sea crawfish.

From the first gray of dawn
The child, looking at the dwindling horizon,
Felt a mysterious sorrow
On the way home, seized by grandmother's hands.

Grandmother, why must I stay here alone?
What!
Your mother went to the land of the sunrise
Crossing over that sea,
No, was it a sun-setting land?

The child was brought up, letting out a big burp
In the blue water of the east sea,
Looking the sunrise
Without omitting one day.

Later on,
At a noisy morning market
The child rose high into the air
With a pure mind.

우리 아빠

아빠
병아리는 물 마시고
하늘을 보지요

나는
물 마시고
아빠를 보지요

나는
물 마시고
아빠를 보는데

아빠는
술 드시고 눈물을 흘려요

아빠는
분단된 조국의 현실이예요
아빠는
술 드시면 눈물을 흘려요

나는 물 마시고
아빠를 보는데

아빠는 술 드시면
눈물을 흘리고

눈물이 아직
마르지 않은 조국에
아빠는 가시고
내가 울어요

아빠
병아리는
물 마시고 하늘을 보는데

어쩌면
나도 물 마시고
하늘을 보아요

My Daddy

Daddy
Chicken sips water
And looks at the sky.

I
Drink water
And look at daddy,

Daddy
Drinks wine and sheds tears.

Daddy
Is the actuality of the divided fatherland.
Daddy
Sheds tears drinking wine.

I drink water
And l see daddy,
Daddy sheds tears
Drinking wine.

In the fatherland,
Yet suffused with tears,
Daddy passed away,
And I cry.

Daddy
Chicken
Sips and looks at the sky,

Somehow,
I also drink water,
And look at the sky.

DMZ에서

하늘도
탄환의 연기가 남아
전쟁의 스모그가 뿌우연
그곳에는
봄날의 꿈틀거리는 생명이
사화산처럼 정지되어
그렇게 차디찼다.

나무의 정령은
반목하고 증오하는
형제의 총부리 앞에 정기를 잃고
보랏빛 라일락 나무는
향기 없는 서름한 움직임만
DMZ를 휘돌아 부는
봄바람에 날렸다.

아버지의 아버지는
이미 그곳에
묻히시고
아버지는
해맑은 청년으로
남하하여
육십여 년, 북녘 하늘만 바라다

돌아가시고
오늘 역사의 능선을 따라
나 이곳에 왔다.

눈앞에 펄렁이는
인공기를 보며
내 가슴속에
각인된
태극기에 대한 맹서는
두 개의 이념을 화해시키지
못했다.

무덤 속같이 고요한 이곳
자유의 마을에
장전된 총알의 긴장을
느끼며
두 시간짜리 짧은 영화 속에서
깨어났다.

어쩌면
영원히—,
통일을 의심하며
답답한 가슴에
초조히
빈 하늘만
바라본다.

At the DMZ

At the spot,
Around which even the sky
Seems to have the smoke of bullets
And the blurred smog of war,
The wiggling life of spring
Is suspended like a dead volcano,
And so cold.

The spirits of trees
Lose their minds before the muzzle of brothers' guns
Being hostile to one another, hating….
And the violet lilac
Waves in the spring wind
Flapping around the DMZ,
Only with strange moves without fragrance.

The father of daddy
Already buried at that spot,
Daddy
As a fine young man,
Walked down to the south
Looking at the northern sky for about 60 years,
Before passing away.
Today,

I came here
Along the ridge–line of history.

Looking at the flag of North Korea
Waving before my eyes,
Even my allegiance to our national flag of Korea
Carved a seal in my heart,
I can't be reconciled to two ideologies.

In this place,
Feeling
The tension of a charged bullet,
I got up
During short the 2 hours' film.

Somehow,
Forever—,
Doubting our unification of North and South,
I look
Only at the vacant sky,
Fretfully, in an anxious state of mind.

소나무

우러러보라
저 높은 산 정상에 비바람, 찬 눈보라에도
꺾이지 않고
고고한 기상으로 서 있는
그를,

내 조국 깊은 산 정상에
모진 풍파 속에
휘어지고 꺾이우고
뿌리째 없어질 위기에도

그 곧은 생명력은
바위를 뚫고
세상의 정기(精氣)를 가슴 깊이
새겨 내 조국 강토를 지켜온
그를,

눈 내리는
고독한 밤,
나는
흰 눈 되어 그를 맞으리
그의 시린 몸뚱이를

하얀 솜이불로 덮어주고
어느덧
겨울이 지나
봄날
아련한 열기 속에
허리를 펴고 싶어,

저 높은 산 정상에
소나무는 어쩔 수 없는
슬픔을 느낀다

내가 그에게
말해주리

"훌륭했다 소나무여
비록 강풍에 견디지 못하고
휘어진 네 육신 위에
난 작은 싹으로,
크게 될 어린 나무로 자라나리
그대 뿌리를 딛고서
바위를 뚫고 일어선
억센 네 생명력을
나 어린 나무 되어
이어가리—"

A Pine Tree

Look up to
Him,
Standing rootedly in lofty solitude,
In spite of being hit hard by rain and snow storms
On the summit of that high mountain,
Without getting broken off,

Irrespective of the crisis,
Being bent, and broken off,
Staying rooted even in the rough wind and waves
On the summit of the deep mountain in my fatherland,

The upright power of life
Piercing a rock,
Has protected the rivers and mountains of our fatherland
Taking the true spirit in his mind,

In the lonely,
Snowing night
I
Will greet him
As white snow coating it,
And cover his naked body
With the white cotton quilt

In no time at all.
Upon a spring day
After the winter has passed,
In the vague hot air
He would like to spread his waist.

The pine tree
Feels inevitable sadness
On the peak of the high mountain.
I will
Talk to him,

"Pine tree! You did great things.
Even as your body curved
Against the unbearable strong winds
As a young seedling.
I will grow into a big tree in the future
And I will inherit the strong living power you had
As a young small tree
Because of your inflexible roots
Piercing the rock—"

제2부

끝없이 흐르는 강

황토를 품에 안고
흐르는 황하를 보셨나요?

무서운 악어가
꼬리 친다는
아마존의 푸른 강을 보셨나요?

당신의 강물을 얘기해 주세요

당신의 강에는
밤이면 밤마다
부엉새 찾아와 울었고

달무리 지는 밤에는
갈대밭 속에
원앙이도 숨어 산다는,

당신 인생의
도화선이 된
인연의 강을
얘기해 주세요

The River Flowing Endlessly

Have you ever seen the running Yellow River,
Carrying yellow soil in its bosom?

Have you ever seen the blue Amazon River,
In which the cruel crocodiles
Are wagging their tails?

Tell me of your river story.

On your river
Night after night,
The owl hoots there,

During the moonlit night
In the field of reeds
A couple of love-birds are living,

Tell me
Has the river of Karma,
Given rise to your life?

덕행의 보루(堡壘)

때론, 범람하는 강물 위에
거세게 내리는 빗줄기처럼
상처받은 내 마음은 외로웠었다

아우성치는 나의 가난한 심사여

빗소리도 은근한
봄날의 비내림이나

잎새 위에 촉촉이 스며드는
아침 열 시에 내리는 여름비로
오셔라

조물주를 경배하는
가을비의 달콤함으로 오셔라

본심은 다정함인데
여린 가슴을 찢고 가버리는
섭섭한 인심이라도

돌아보면
너와 나

하늘과 땅 사이
마음 기댈 곳 없어
방황하는 나그네
…
강가에 둑을 쌓으리라
더 높게 쌓으리라

범람하는 강물 위에
거세게 내리는 빗줄기 같던
나의 마음이여,

생명을 키우는
저 찬란한 강물의
흐름이여!

A Fortress of Virtue

Sometimes, upon the overflowing river
Like great streaks of rain
My wounded mind was lonesome.

My poor, crying heart!

Raining down on a spring day,
With its sound so silent,

Come down
As a summer rain at 10 o'clock in the morning
That is fully soaking into the leaves.

Come down with your sweetness of autumn rain
As serving the Creator.

My true self is tenderness,
But in spite of the regretful man's mind
That tore a feeble heart away,

Reflecting upon the past,
You and I,
Between the heaven and the earth
Are wandering strangers

Who can't rely on others for help
...
I will build the bank of the river,
And pile it up highly.

My heart!
Pouring down as strong streaks of rain
Upon the overflowing river,

The flow
Of that brilliant river water,
Nurturing up all life!

나의 도요새

그이는 날 보고 새도우 체이셔(shadow chaser)라고 했다.
그이는 날 보고 드림 매니아(dream maniac)라고 했다.
그러나
그이는 나의 비상(飛上)을 안다.

구구거리는 비둘기 떼 속에
한 마리 도요새가, 빙글대는 여름 한낮의
태양을 향하여 날개를 쳤다.

해는 아득하고
이제금 날 저물어 비들기들은
어울려 제 둥지를 찾는데

나의 외로운 도요새는 먼—데
석양을 그린다.

다시는
이 강가에서 목을 축이지 않겠노라
다짐하지만
제 그림자를 남기고 떠난 그 자리에
필시 나의 도요새는 다시 오리라…

그이는 날 보고 새도우 체이셔라고 했다.
그이는 날 보고 드림 매니아라고 했다.
그러나 나의 외로운 도요새는
내가 언제나 비상을 꿈꾸는
영원한 방랑자라는 것을

나의 외로운 도요새는
알고 있다.

My Snipe

He said that I was a shadow chaser.
He said that I was a dream maniac.
But
He knows my soaring.

One snipe among the group of cooing pigeons
Flapped its wings toward the sun,
At high noon of an idle summer.

The sun is far off.
Now it grows dark and the pigeons

Look for their nests together,

My lonesome snipe
Pines for the far sunset.

Though my snipe vows,
That he will never again
Wet his whistle in this river,
At the place where he left his shadow behind,
Surely my snipe will come back again…

He said that I was a shadow chaser;
He said that I was a dream maniac.
But my lonesome snipe
Knows that I am a eternal wanderer
Dreaming of flight afar

My snipe knows well
How high I want to soar up.

나비와 내가

나비와 내가
앞서거니 뒤서거니
콧노래를 부르며
개울가를 걷는다

들꽃은 뜨건 태양 아래
샛노랗게 피어서고
나비는 그 서슬이 싫여
되려 나를 쫓아오네

사르르 날갯짓도 부드러운
나비는 손가락에 앉아서
섬섬옥수도 아닌데
다정한 마음이 좋았나 보다

Butterfly and I

A butterfly and I
Walk along a stream,
Crooning,
Passing or going ahead of each other in turn.

The field flowers under the hot sun
Bloom in yellow.
The butterfly dislikes its impetuosity,
And would rather follow me.

The butterfly, flapping so tenderly his wings
Sits on my fingers
Which aren't delicate,
Seems to enjoy my sweet heart.

지난날

최영섭 작곡

말없이 강가를 나 홀로 거닐면
물새 한 마리 갈꽃 새에 몸을 감추고
외로운 마음에 그윽히 노래 부르면
먼 산 그림자 강물에 어린다

별떨기 피어나는 하늘에는
어린 적 동무 얼굴 날 찾는 듯 반짝이고
지난날 우리의 우정이 강물 따라 흐른다

지난날 우리의 언약이
강물 따라 흐른다

아 아 그리움아 세월은 흘러
우리의 언약이 강물 따라 흐른다

Yesterday

composed by Choi Young-seup

When I am walking silently along the river in solitude,
One water-bird hides among the reeds,
Singing secretly a song with a lonesome heart,
The shadow of the far mountain hangs around the river.

In the sky the star-flowers bloom,
My friend's face in childhood is glistening, as if looking for me.
Our friendship in days if old flows along the river.

Our vows made in past days
Run along the river.

O, O, the yearning! As time passes by,
Our vows flow along the river together.

추억

홍제천 산책길을
홀로 걷자니
노오란 수선화는 벌써 피었고
물비린내 어린 시절
바다 같아라

금붕어의 비늘처럼
물결이 일고
목이 긴 클로버 하얀 꽃망울이
옛 생각에 잠기게 하네

풀꽃반지 만들던
그날 그 머언 날
꽃보다 고운님은 아—아—
흐르는 저 강물 따라
돌아오지 않네

A Retrospect

When I was taking a walk alone
Along a strolling lane of Hongjecheon,
The yellow narcissus were already in bloom,
And its smell seems to be
The sea of my childhood.

It moves in waves
Like a goldfish's scales,
And the white flower bud of a long-necked clover
Absorbs me in old thoughts.

In those days, the old days
We made flower-rings for each other.
My sweetheart's love was sweeter than flowers,
Ah—ah— It flew afar
Along that running river.

사랑의 종이 되리

이안삼 작곡

만약에 내가
다시 사랑을 한다면
내 님의 빛나는 눈동자에
언뜻 어린 한 방울 눈물이 되리

내 님의 옷깃을 스치고
지나가는 부드런 바람이 되리

내 님은 날 아시려나
눈물방울 떨어지고
바람 되어 사라지는
날 아시려나

만약에 내가
다시 사랑을 한다면
내 님의 가슴 속에 울려퍼지는
사랑의 종이 되리

내 님이 날 아시듯
나는 내 님 곁에
가만히 맴도는
종소리의 울림이 되리

I Will Be A Bell For Love

composed by Lee An-sam

If I
Fall in love again,
I will be a drop of a tender tear
On the shining eyes of my lover.

And I will be a soft wind
Brushing by my lover's dress collar.

Will my lover recognize me,
Me, shedding tears,
Remember me,
Disappearing as if I had become the wind?

If I
Fall in love again,
I will become a bell
Echoing out in my lover's heart.

And an echo
I will become, of the bell's sound
Whirling round my lover silently,
As if my sweet heart knows me.

상사(相思)

이안삼 작곡

그대가 이슬만 먹고 사는
한 포기 들꽃이라면, 나는
그대로 인하여
눈물의 밤바다를 헤매이는
한 떨기 별꽃이어라

그대와 나의 만남은
해풍에 스러지는
물결과도 같아라
그대를 바라는 나의 마음은
산들바람에 흔들리는 꽃잎의
수줍음인 것을…

분주한 여름은
이 끝없는 인연의 백사장에
우리를 남겨두고 모래알을 안고 달아나는
저 지혜로운 조수(潮水)와 같구나

오—
오늘도 너의
소슬한 몸짓에
나는 운다

Reciprocal Affection

composed by Lee An-sam

If you are a field flower plant
Only living on dew,
On account of you, I
Would like to be a bunch of star–flowers
Wandering about the night a sea of tears.

The meeting of you and I
Is like waves
Breaking by a sea wind.
My heart desiring you
Is the shame of the flower's leaf
Shaken by a gentle breeze…

The busy summer
Is like that wise tides
Running away with the sands,
Leaving us at the endless white sands of karma.

O—
Today
I weep
For your desolate gesture.

메아리

내가 아직 어렸을 때
나는 그대를 불렀네
그리움과 기다림의 간곡한 노래—

내가 어른이 되었더니
메아리도 목소리에
시름이 묻어 있네

아— 아—

밤이나 낮이나
내 맘 속에 부딪고 돌아오는
사랑의 메아리여

그댈 부르네
메아리도 그대 찾아 머언 먼 시절로
돌아가고파…… .

An Echo

When I was young,
I sang to you,
In a cordial song of yearning and waiting.

After I became an adult
I found the voice
That was an echo smeared with griefs.

Ah— Ah—

Love's echo!
Hitting against my mind and resounding
Day and night,

I sing to you.
The echo also seeking for you,
Wants to come back for the season far away…….

소요지경

갈매기 한 마리
파도 따라 넘실댄다

물 아래 그림자도
파도 따라 출렁댄다

잠깐
세상 구경나온 꼴뚜기 갑자기
먹총을 쏘아

갈매기 눈멀었다
꼴뚜기 사냥에

Rambling Mood

One sea gull
Moves on the waves.

Its shadow under water
Surges after the waves.

One moment
An octopus who came out to see the world
Suddenly shot Indian ink.

The sea gull was blind
To hunting octopuses.

제3부

흘러라 내 마음의 강물이여

최영섭 작곡

흐르는 내 마음의 잔잔한 강물은
청자빛 하늘색 구름을 담고
꽃향기 찾아 날아가는 범나비
그림자 담고 그림자 담고

내 마음의 강물은 긴 목 해오라기
두리번거리는 가련한 생명을 담고

흐르는 내 마음의 강물은
청자빛 하늘색 몸매 머얼리 쪽빛 바다
돛단배 하나에 아련히 머문다
흘러라 흘러라 내 마음의 강물이여

Flow, River of my Heart!

composed by Choi Young-seup

The silent river flowing in my heart
With celadon green clouds,
Is like a swallowtail looking for fragrant flowers
With his shadow, and with his shadow.

The river of my heart is a slender white heron,
With a restless, poor life.

The calm river flowing in my heart
Like the celadon green on the far indigo sea
Stays dimly as a sailboat,
Flow, flow, the river of my heart.

서울 이야기

발아래 굽어본다
어느 은하계인가

별 초롱 꿈 초롱
지금 어드메쯤
잠투정 어린 아기
엄마 품이 그리운데
엄닐랑 일터에 나가 아니 돌아오는,
서울은
잠이 없어라

아기야
되려 네가 엄닐 용서해
다고

Seoul Story

I look down below my feet
Is it any galaxy?

A limpid star, a limpid dream,
A little baby getting fretful before sleep
Yearning for its mommy's breast.
Seoul
Where its mom hasn't come back yet,
Always lies awake.

Baby,
Rather forgive your mom.

서울에 산다

사람들의 다급한 발걸음
부딪고 아파하고
헤어진다
거리에는
요염한 옷가지들
싸구려 화장품
마네킹에나 어울리는
가냘픈 하이힐
넘쳐나는,

까마득한 고층 아파트
손바닥만한 방
이 집도 저 집 같고
저 집도 그 집 같으니
어려울사
할아버지 할머니
고향 그리다 지치셨다
파도,
파도,
파도!
파도!
파도!

파도!
파도!
파도!
뱃고동
뚜— 우—

Living in Seoul

People in Seoul
Bump into other people while going along on their business,
And live separately, feeling the pain.
The streets
Are brimful
The colorful clothes,
Cheap cosmetics
With girls' high heels
Being suitable for mannequins,

The miniature little rooms
In the high many storied apartment buildings,
This house looks like that one,

So it's very difficult
For grand father and grand mother
To find it,
And they became tired out in pining for their home.
Waves,
Waves,
Waves!
Waves!
Waves!
Waves!
Waves!
Waves!
The Boat Whistle
Toot— toot—

보호받는 풍경

물속에는 파—란 이끼들이
바람 따라 가볍게
살랑댄다

목을 길게 빼고 진달래꽃이
계곡물 위으로 얼굴을 비춘다
제 모습에 도취되어

세상의 여인네들이
저마다 자신의 거울을 보며
화장을 하듯이

꽃들도 바람결에
얼굴을 뽐내며
한 잎 두 잎

계곡물 위에 떨어져
복사꽃잎 떠 오는 무릉도원이
과연 이곳이 아닐까—

그대와 내가
이곳을 사랑하여 다시 찾는다면

이 신비한 비경은

봄날이 소낙비에 밀리어 가듯
사라질 줄
누가 알까…

Protected Scenery

The green mosses in water
Blow gently
On the wind.

The azaleas sticking out their long necks
Reflect their faces over the stream of the valley
Stimulating with their looks.

Like the women of the world
Make up their own faces
Looking at a mirror,

One or two petals
Of the flowers on the wind

Taking pride in their faces,

Fell on the stream of the valley.
So the place with peach blossoms floating on it
Really isn't a utopia?

If you and I
Love this spot and look for it again,
This mysterious landscape

No body knows
That will disappear
Like the spring season is swept along by a shower.

멍에

대관령 목장의 소떼들은
멍에를 씌우지 않았는데
우리 집 음메소는 멍에를 짊어졌다.

우리 집 음메소가 허약한 아버지를
위하여 자청한 것이 아니다
그도 때로는 도리질을 하고 싶고,

구름이 영을 넘는 한여름에는
대관령에 사는 친구들처럼
넙죽 엎드려 싱긋 풀 향기에 취하고도 싶다.

그러나 우리 집 음메소는 봄, 여름, 가을
지나 겨울이 올 때까지
아버지가 씌어놓은 멍에에 갇혀

지친 다리를 절며
아버지가 잡아끄는 대로 끌려 끌려
한세상을 살다 죽었다.

아버진 아무 미련 없이
고깃국을 드신다.

나도 어쩌면
아버지로 인하여 나서, 자라고,
아버지가 씌어놓은 인생의 멍에를 짊어진,
불쌍한 내 친구의 우울한
눈빛을 닮아간다.

우리 집 음메소와 나는
아버지를 남몰래 미워했다.
지금도 하늘 저편에 어둠이 짙어오면
나는 외양간에 갇힌
우리 집 음메소처럼

나의 아틀리에 숨어
무심히 하늘의 별을 본다……

A Yoke

Groups of cows in the ranch of Daekwanryung
Are not yoked,
But our cow is under a yoke.

It was not what our cow wanted, to be put in a yoke
By our weak father,
But sometimes he wanted to show an unpleasant sign,

In midsummer when the clouds passed over the high mountain,
Our cow wanted to get exhilarated in the fresh grass fragrance
Lying flat on the grass field like the friends in Daekwanryung.

But our cow through all seasons,
Spring, summer, autumn, and winter,
Having a yoke put on him,

Drags his tired feet
Being taken to work hard like this by father,
And died in a way too pitiful to tell.

However, father takes the cow's meat
Without any regret.
Perhaps I
Was born, raised by father,
With life's yoke packed on me by father,
Also take after the melancholic eyes
Of my poor friend's eyes.

Our cow and I
Hated father secretly.
Now at the sundown beyond the sky,
Like our little cow
Confined to the stable,

I look at the stars in the sky unconcernedly,
Hidden in my studio.

여름

집짓는 소리 목(目)전에
분주하고 머리 위엔 작열하는 태양

키 작은 노인이
점(占)으로 앉아 후딱 말해버린 여름

내가
저 하늘의 해보다
먼저 불타고
한 줌 흙거름이 될까

The Summer

The sounds of house building
Are busy under a scorching sun,

An old fortuneteller of small stature
Told of the summer simply.

How can I
Burn ahead
Before the sun on that sky, and
Return to a handful of earth's manure!

여름 정경

정오가 되면
뜨끈뜨끈한 연무
뽀오얀 태양 속으로
잠적해 버린
집 짓는 사람들,

자장면 배달하는 아이는
낡은 오토바이를 몰고
아득한 기억 속에
멀어져간다.

언 땅 속에서 악전고투하던
겨울날의 우리들,
가을에는 하늘 끝에서부터
유랑의 무리처럼
떠돌고
텃밭엔 이미 남모르게
우거진 잡초……

다른 이들이
늘어진 시계추처럼
지쳐 있을 때

무(無)와 존재함이
멈추어 있는
이 우주 공간 속에서
나는,
한순간의 티끌로
사라지기 싫었다.

A Summer Sketch

At high noon
In the warm smog and fog,
The persons
Who were building a house,
Hide from the glaring sun.

The boy
Who was delivering Jajangmyeon*,
Driving an old motorcycle,
Disappears from far memory.

We, on the winter day,
Struggled desperately upon the frozen ground,

Wandered about
Like a group of vagabonds
From the end of sky in autumn
And the rank weeds
Already grown secretly at the family garden……

When other people
Are tired out,
Like a late clock's pendulum,
In this space of the universe
Where the void and existence
Are stopping
I,
Resent having to return
To the dust of a moment.

*Jajangmyeon : a kind of noodle.

가을 서정

봄 동산의 두견이는
진홍 빛깔 애기 씨 마음이고

여름 시냇가에 물고기 쫓는 아이들
물보라 일으키며 만드는 무지개
동심은 사랑스럽다

도시의 포도 위에서는 플라타너스,
잎새 홀로서 떨어진다
너와 나의 연분의 정도
끊어지고
요란했던 인간사 열기도
이제는 식었어라
혼자 가는 길
지금 나 죽어 한 줌
흙거름 되었다가 다시
봄 동산 진달래로 피어날까…
가을은 회생을 기약하고 싶다

산천에 흰 눈 덮이면
그때사 침묵하리라

Song of Autumn

A cuckoo in the spring garden
Is as scarlet as a baby's heart,

Little boys catching fishes,
And a rainbow made in the rising spray of water
Are in the lovely juvenile mind.

The sycamore on the pavement in the center of the city,
Its leaves fall alone.
The predestined bond between you and I
Is cut
And the noisy human passion
Also gets cold.
While making a road myself,
Now I return to a handful of dust
Into the ground.
Can I bloom as an azalea again in the spring garden…
I want the promise of returning to life in Autumn.

When mountains and rivers are covered with white snow
Then I will keep silent.

허수아비

허수아비가
있거나 말거나
메뚜기는 뛰어다니고
참새는 날아다녀요

메뚜기와 참새도
세태를 탐인지
꾀가 많아졌어요

허수아비는 정말
할 일이 없어요
참새가 허수아비 머리에 앉아
콕콕 쪼아도 보고
옷소매를 땡겨도 보아도
허수아비는 눈물이 없어요

그러나
허수아비는
생각하지요
태어나지 말 것을
무가치한 인생이여!

만약 허수아비 같은 슬픔을 가진
사람이라면 큰 소리로 말하세요
훠———이
훠———이
나는 곡식을 지키는 허수아비
나는 그리움의 허수아비
나는 시를 쓴다네
훠———이
훠———이

The Scarecrow

Without minding the scarecrow at all,
The locusts run here and there;
The sparrows fly too.

The locusts and sparrows
Are full of tricks,
As if they reflect social conditions.

The scarecrow really
Has nothing to do.

The sparrow sits on his head
And pecks at it,
Pulling his sleeve.
None the less, the scarecrow has no tears.

But
The scarecrow
Wishes
It had not been born.
O, worthless life!

If we feel such sadness as the scarecrow,
Say like this loudly:
'Get———away'
'Get———away'
I am a scarecrow keeping grains,
I am a scarecrow of yearning.
I am writing a poem,
'Get———away'
'Get———away'

홀로 있는 시간

나는
내 이름 석 자를
손가락에 힘껏 힘주어 적으며
세상의 온갖 축복의 말로써
마음에 새긴다
그러나
홀로 있는 시간이
하루 이십사 시간
일 년이 지나고…
이 년이 지나고…
또 다시
새해가
밝아 왔다
과연
나는
내 이름 석 자를
어떻게 가꿀 것인가
언제나
홀로 있는 시간…
무엇인지 모르나 나는
무엇인가를 향하고 있으며
한밤중에 잠 깨어

매무새를 단정히 갖추고
책상 앞에 앉아
변함없는 하루를
반성하고,
반성하고,
또 반성한다
하노라면
나의 앞날은
태양이 가득히 비치고
어느 날
나는
내 이름 석 자에
꾸짖은
많은 말들을 기억한
한 그루
어진 묘목이
될 것만 같다

홀로 있는 시간,
고통의 날이 지나면
행복의 날이
온다고 했느니

세월아!
잠자코
네 갈 길로 가거라

나는 호올로
외로운 작업에
하루해가
또
저물었다

An Hour by Myself

I
Write three words of my name
By the sheer strength of my fingers,
And this carves it on my mind
As a congratulatory speech.
But
The hour by myself
Becomes twenty-four hours,
One year passes···
Two years pass···
And again
The new year
Dawned.
Really!
How can I
Use the three words of my name?
Always
The hour by myself comes···
I don't know
What is it, but I tend toward something,
Waking up at night
Adjusting my dress neatly,
And sit before the table
To reflect on,

To reflect on,
And again to reflect on
The unvarying day.
If I go on reflecting,
My future
Will be filled with sunlight;
And one day
I think
That I may become
A root of
The wise sapling
Which remembered its scolding
Like the three words of my name.

The hour by myself,
Someone said,
If the painful day has passed,
The happy day would truly come.
O, time!
Silently
Go your way as you like.

While working
By myself,
Again
One day has come to a close.

제4부

산길에서

아침 해가
동녘 하늘을 비집고 나오려는
이맘때면

아직 가시지 않은 어둠이
큰 미륵바위 뒤에서
짓궂게 웃는다

괜스레
부끄러운 생각에
풀포기를 뜯는다

이슬은
노오란 우산 위에 떨어졌다
사방으로 튀어 달아나는
빗방울처럼

머얼리
머얼리로
흔들어 보냈다

산을 오르는
사람들은
매양 그 얼굴이 똑같지만

오늘은 햇님같이
발그레한 내 얼굴을
아무도 모르신다

In the Mountain Path

At the time
When the morning sun tries to come out
Splitting open the eastern sky,

Darkness that hasn't been replaced by the dawn yet,
Laughs annoyingly
Behind a big stone statue of Buddha.

In vain
I take apart grasses
For shame.

Dews
Drop on the yellow umbrella,
Like raindrops dripping on all sides,

Far away
Far away,
Shaking them to send.

Though climbers
Are always just alike
In their faces,

Today nobody knows
A face as flushed as mine
Like the sun.

어느 봄날 아침

세상은 뽀오얀 우유빛
안개에 잠기고
담장을 타고 흐드러진
개나리 꽃잎에도

내 사랑하는 사람의
눈빛처럼 온화한
정분이 감돈다
아— 아— 어여뻐라
봄날은 저기 저 부드러운 안개 속으로 날아간
새의 깃털 속에서 반짝이고

부시시 잠깬 내 님의
고운 눈꺼풀 위에
살며시 내려앉은 사월의
햇볕처럼
따스한 미소로부터
나에게로 온단다.

One Morning of A Spring Day

The world sinks
In the clear milky fog,
And also in the fetching sound of the golden bell
Climbing over the wall,

The soft sentiments,
Like my loving sweetheart
Remain.
Ah— ah— it's beautiful,
The spring day is shining
In the bird's feathers as it flew off into that soft fog,

Like the sunlight sat quietly
On the pretty eyebrow of my sweetheart
Awakening from his bed gently,
As April
Comes up to me
From its mild smile.

봄의 풍광

몸부림치며 견뎌온
잔인한 겨울의 고독
늪에서는 잠자던 물뱀이
꼬리를 흔들며 유영한다

진줏빛깔 은은한
하늘가에
오늘도 꽃편지 같은
개나리 순이 연연히
물오른다

때론 격렬하게 가지를 떨고
때론 조급히 꽃 피었다
반지보다 작은 나의 별에도
봄이 왔다

산능선을 따라 깊은 골짜기에는
햇볕도 발길을 주춤하는 곳
머잖아 어른 키만 한 대마가 울창하고
물미나리 질세라 어깨를 휘청거릴 때를
기약하며

봄이여!
수많은 빛깔의 계절이여!
하늘의 별무리보다 아름다운
지상의 엘레우시스 제전*에
그대도 어서 달려와
축배를 들어라

* 엘레시우스 제전 : 곡식의 여신 데메테르를 경배하는 제전 의식.

A Beautiful Spring

In the cruel aloneness
That all things have been survived strugglingly,
The sleeping water snake in the marsh
Is swimming in the water, shaking his tail.

Today, at the edge
Of the pearly white-colored sky
The sap's golden bell's bud,
Like a flower's letter,

Begins to rise.

Sometimes shivering its branches violently,
Sometimes blooming earlier.
Spring has come also
In my star, smaller than a ring.

Spring!
The season of numerous colors!
You, come quickly to Eleusinian Mysteries*
And drink a toast
For the ritual in the early more beautiful
Than many a star in the heavens.

*Eleusinian Mysteries : Some kinds of ritual for Demeter, the goddess of agriculture in Greek mythology. Demeter is the mother of Persephone.

고양이

봄 햇살 아래 누워
지나간 영화를 꿈꾼다
밤이 되면 어둠을 향하여
갓난아기처럼 애설피 울었다

가장 고결한 품위를
사뿐한 네 발 끝에 감추고
거만한 여왕같이 독무를
연기한다

태생이 영묘하다
너를 두려워하네
너를 두려워하네
교활한 꾀가

오물거리는 주둥이 안에 숨어 있다
가끔씩 입을 열고
권태를 토해내는 저 게으른
울음

누가 너를 인간의 침대 속으로
불러들였는가

누가 너를 엄동설한에
길거리로 방사하였는가

너의 속성도 모르고
그 보드라운 털에 입 맞추는
요염한 여인네의 짝이 되어,
불길한 짐승 같으니!

인간의 탐욕과 욕정에서
비롯된 고양이의 팔자

The Cat

Lying under the sunlight
He dreamed about his glory of the past.
At night fell toward darkness
He cried sadly like a baby.

He plays his own part with brilliance,
Like an arrogant queen,
Hiding his noblest dignity
Under the end of his four elastic legs.

His life-giving substance is subtle,
I am afraid of you,
I feel a horror of you.
His cunning trick

Hiding in his mumbling bill.
Opening his mouth often,
The lazy cry
Spews of his boredom,

Who brought you
Into the human bed?
Who expelled you
Out of the street during the severe winter?

You ominous animal!
Kissing his soft furs
Without knowing his generic character,
Like a voluptuous woman's partner,

The cat's destiny
Began with the greed and carnal lust of a human being.

조국

내가 어리석어
아무리 불평해도
한마디 냉정한 말씀도
아니하시는 나의 참된 아버지
나를 낳으신 생부는
내 어리석고 유치한 반란을
차디찬 눈초리로 매질하셨지

나의 참된 아버지
조국은 내가 마음이 어려
아무리 못된 장난과 꾀로
문밖에 소문이 자자해도
잠자코 내게 기다림을 주신 아버지

이제 철이 들어
아버지 조국이라고 한마디
부름만으로도 가슴에 뜨겁게
눈물이 맺히고
소문의 끝도 아득히 먼 세월에
나 자라,
아버지 뜻대로
살고 싶습니다

My Fatherland

As I am silly,
However hard I may complain,
My true father
Doesn't treat me with a cold word.

My own natural father
Whipped my silly and childish defiance
With a stern look.

My true father,
The fatherland sees I am young in mind,
However much the outside-rumor may have been getting around
Through my mischief and tricks,
My true father generously waits for me to come back.

Now being in prosperous days,
Even as I say only one word, 'Fatherland',
Tears come to my eyes in drops
From a burning bosom,
And growing up
While having no relation to the rumors,
Now I want to live
Just as my fatherland expects.

진주

비바람이 몰아친다
내 몸을 적신다
내 맘을 적신다 그리고
나의 상처 난 아픈 가슴에
이방의 진주를 심었다

푸른 빛깔의 진주 씨알을 품고
아픔에 몸부림치며 참고 견뎌온 세월
내리는 비는 내 마음의 진주를 성숙시켰다

저—푸르른 하늘이여
그리움이여 내 마음을 깊게 숨겨 둔
타성의 바다 속에서
나는 이방의 진주를 키웠다
그리고 드디어 그들로부터 해방되었다

하늘과 바다
내가 서 있는 이 땅 위에서
나도 한 알의 진주가 되리라

A Seed of Pearl

Rain and wind blow violently.
They drench my body.
They make my mind wet and
They implant a pearl from an alien country
In my wounded heart.

Over the years that the pearl has taken patience
Struggling in desperate pain, holding its blue-
colored seed in its bosom.
The falling rain has ripened a pearl in my mind.

O, that blue heaven!
O, nostalgia! In the sea of inertia
That hid deeply in my mind
I brought up the pearls of an alien country.
And at last was free from them.

In the heaven and sea,
And on this ground that I stand on,
I will be a seed of pearl.

이유

자명종
나는 자명종
사색의 동굴 나의 방에
오늘도 쉬지 않고 돌아가는
나는 자명종

천지의 정기가 박동하는
새벽이면
북한산 보랏빛 능선 따라
바야흐로 넘어가는
저 하늘의 유성

순결한 나의 님!

지성(至誠)의 마지막 고지
조국에 바치는 나의 정절(貞節)
나의 휘델리티(fidelity)

그분과 내가
남몰래 맺은 언약
위태로운 내 상념의 쪽배를
순풍으로 인도하시는

그분은
그분은 나의 조국,

순결하신 나의 님
나의 조국이여
나도 어진 그대 닮아
자비와 충성을 다짐하며

항상 깨어 있는
나는
조국의 시계
나는 자명종(alarm).

The Reason

An alarm clock.
I am the alarm clock
Turning round without rest in my room,
The cave of thought today.
I am an alarm.

At dawn,

The vitality of heaven and earth is beating,
The falling star in the sky
Along the violet ridges of Mt. Bukhan
Is passing over just now.

An innocent love of mine!
He is the last high land of my honor,
The chastity devoted to my fatherland,
And my fidelity.

The pledge
That he and I made secretly,
And he,
Leading the tiny dangerous boat of my beliefs
In a favorable wind,
Is my fatherland.

An innocent love of mine,
The fatherland!
Vowing sympathy and loyalty to him,
By duplicating your kindness,

I,
Always waking,
A clock of the fatherland,
I am an alarm clock.

그대도 내 맘같이

그대는
아득한 새벽하늘을
날아가는 시간
궁수의 활을 벗어난
살과 같이

해가 뜨면 나는
붉은 망토를 휘감고서
천년만년 그대와 함께
말 없는 기쁨의 순례자이고
싶습니다

금빛 찬란한 아침 해가
나의 항구에 정박할
무렵이면
그대도 내 맘같이

영광된 내일의 메시지를
노래하는 별이 되어
동화처럼 나의 가슴속에서
빛날 것입니다

'그대는 나의
영원한 친구
소망의 기도입니다.'

Also You, Like My Heart

You
Are the time
Flying far away in the sky of dawn,
Like an arrow getting out of an archer's bow.

When the sun rises,
I want to be a silent pilgrim of joy
With you for ever
Displaying the red mantle.

At the time
When the brilliant golden sun of morning
Anchors at my harbor,
Also anchors at yours.
You will be bright
In my heart like a fairy tale,
As a star singing
A glorious message of the future.

'You are
The prayer of hope,
The friend of my soul.'

영원히

어떤 때는 하늘을 보고
어떤 때는 꽃잎을 뜯고
어떤 때는 진리를 구하며
어떤 때는 시를 썼다

하늘을 바랄 땐
두 손을 가슴에 모두고
바다를 바랄 땐
수평선의 갈매기를 보며
조용하고 우아한 나래짓도 그렸다

그대를 찾으려고
숲 속에서 길 잃은 아이처럼
나무그루를 셈하기도 하였고
벼랑 위에 서서
애절한
메아리를 만들어 보기도 하였다

해빙하는 강물처럼
나지막이 울기도 하였다
내가 얼마나 오랜 시간 속을
우주를 방황하는 떠돌이별로

살아왔던가

그대를 찾기 위하여
나의 신앙 속에는
만 가지 애니미즘과 윤회와,
창조의 신 하나님을 찬미할 줄
나 이미 알았구나

Forever

Sometimes I look at heaven,
Sometimes I look at a flower's petal,
Sometimes I look for truth,
Sometimes I write a poem.

Praying toward heaven
I gathered two hands to my bosom,
Desiring the sea,
I looked at the sea gull on the horizon,
And I traced the gentle and elegant movement of her wing.

To look for you
Like a child losing his way in the woods,
I counted trees,
And made a sad echo
Standing on the cliff.

I also wept rather softly.
How long had I lived
Through time as a vagabond star
Roaming in the universe?

In order to find you
In my faith,
I already knew
Ten thousand philosophies and theories of reincarnation,
The creator, the God to praise.

종달새

나의 새벽은
시계 침의 꼭대기에 있습니다
상쾌한 아침입니다
세상이 고요히
잠이 든 때
나와 당신만이 존재하듯
사위는 깜깜한 밤입니다

나의 새벽은
당신의 약속
나와 더불어 당신은
새벽을 가장 먼저 알리는
종달새

당신은 깜깜한 밤하늘을
떠받드는
아틀라스 신(神)
나와 더불어
당신은 새벽을 가장
먼저 알리는 종달새

당신은 나의 가슴에
훌륭히 빛나는
승리의 마스코트입니다

The Lark

My dawn
Comes from the top of the watch's hands.
It is fresh morning.
When the world is concealed silently in darkness,
As if only you and I exist,
Like dark night around us.

My dawn
Is your promise.
You with me
Are the lark
That informs us of the dawn first of all.

You are the god, Atlas,
Who holds up
The dark night of heaven.

You with me
Are the lark
Who reports the dawn first of all.

You are
The mascot of victory
Shining splendidly in my bosom.

사랑의 종이 되리

(I Will Be A Bell For Love)

이독밀 시
이안삼 곡

mf
f
면 내 님 의 빛 나 는 눈 동 자 에
면 내 님 의 빛 나 는 눈 동 자 에
언 뜻 어 린 한 방 울 눈 물 되 리 내 님 의 옷 깃 을 스 치 고
언 뜻 어 린 한 방 울 눈 물 되 리 내 님 의 옷 깃 을 스 치 고
mp
지 나 가 는 부 드 런 바 람 되 리 내 님 의 가 슴 속 에 울 려 퍼 지 는
지 나 가 는 부 드 런 바 람 되 리 내 님 의 가 슴 속 에 울 려 퍼 지 는

사 랑 의종 이 되 리
사 랑 의종 이 되 리
아 내 님 은 날 아 시 려
아 내_님 은 날 아 시 려

32
fff
a tempo
나 눈 물 방 울 떨 어 지 고 바 람 되 어 사 라 지 는 나 아
나 가__ 만 히 맴____ 도____ 는 종__ 소__ 리 울
35
2절 →
시 려 나 나
림 되 리 라 라

문학세계대표작가선 708

종달새(The Lark)

이독밀 한영대역시집

인쇄 1판 1쇄 2014년 2월 28일
발행 1판 1쇄 2014년 3월 7일

지 은 이 : 이독밀
펴 낸 이 : 金天雨
펴 낸 곳 : 도서출판 天雨
등 록 : 1992. 2. 15. 제1-1307호
주 소 : 서울시 성동구 무학봉28길 6(하왕십리동 966-23) 금용빌딩 2F
전 화 : 02)2298-7661
팩 스 : 02)2298-7665
http://www.moonhaknet.com
E-mail : chunwo@hanmail.net

값 8,000원

ISBN 978-89-7954-560-9